Table of Contents:

Acknowledgements

Nadia

Michelle

Ladele

The Group Discussion

Nicolette

Rosebud

Joan

Duane

Acknowledgements

The following is a compilation of true stories of single mothers who belong to a Non-Profit Organization called Undercover Heroes.

I wanted to thank everyone involved in the production of this work since without the input and effort of everyone involved, this would not have been possible.

Thank you all for making this a reality.

To my family and friends who have supported me through the years, I thank you.

Nadia

The way I met Nadia was quite serendipitous. I've been told that the Universe is too mathematical to make mistakes. In this case I'm inclined to agree. The decisions we make affect our lives and in turn affect the lives of the people around us. When we make choices and take action, those actions and choices have an impact on the world around us and form this giant stage of dominoes set up to knock into each other and eventually create a beautiful picture viewed from a higher vantage point. Once you see how your words, actions and choices begin to come alive and take shape in the form of bonds, organizations and relationships, it is then that upon looking back, you realize that you can have an effect on your physical reality and make things happen, simply by making a choice to make a difference.

Nadia chose to make a difference. We found ourselves having coffee after numerous messages and voice notes trying to organize the meeting which would lead to the beginning of this collection of real stories about the lives of strong and brave women who face the daily uphill battle of being single mothers. Nadia had kicked off her Non – Profit Organization in 2019 which was, and still is, geared towards single parenting.

Highlighting the fact that it's not easy and those who do so need to be aware that they are not **alone** in their struggles, though at times it may seem that way.

My coffee was gone within minutes but it hit hard and I was intrigued and awestruck by the story that I was listening to first hand knowing that there would be more to come. The tale of how we arrived at that moment was through connections. After founding the organization, Nadia met many single parents including single fathers. One of them happen to be my best friend who discovered her through the girlfriend of a mutual friend of ours. When Nadia expressed her idea for compiling a book to tell the stories of the parents in her organization, she was on the phone with him and he blurted out that he knew a published Author personally and as the universe would have it, I walked into his living room while they were on that call. This is the kind of thing that if it were scripted it would seem fake however, that is exactly what happened. Months later after the dust of lockdown, day jobs and other things called life had settled, Nadia reached out to me once again and I was honoured to take on the task of interviewing and compiling the stories of these courageous souls and what they had to say. There are many other things that were discussed and I will not be boring you with the details. Nadia did however decide that she would offer her own tale to kick things off. Shall we…

I was interested to know and hear the back story of the brave women who tackled the perilous journey of being a single mother. Having the opportunity to hear their stories let alone write about them was and is an honour. I devised a series of questions which I felt, people who were not in their position would like to know, as well as exploratory questions on how their lives got to the point which they found themselves in.

Taking another sip of a delicious expresso, I whipped out my list of questions and a notepad. Nadia had never been interviewed and did extremely well in my opinion as she sipped her Latte in a takeaway cup because the barista said that for that size, they didn't have any ceramics for *in house enjoyment*.

The name **Undercover Heroes** was registered in September 2019 and it was in that same year that Nadia miraculously arranged and hosted an event to pamper single parents and reminded them that they **are worth being taken care of.**
The origin of the name came from a thought. *"All single parents wear superhero capes underneath their clothes,"* her point was valid as it was true. The idea had me nodding in agreement as the understanding of the concept made perfect sense. Single parents pull things off for their children everyday having one arm tied behind their back (metaphorically). And that, to me, places them in the Superhero category.

I agreed whole heartedly thinking of the heroes in my own life and the medical workers on the frontline during the pandemic.

Since single mothers are on their own, they do the job of both parents and it can be taxing on the mind, body and soul. Everyone needs a break.

"Take me back to the day the reality set in that you are now a single mother."

I began the interview explaining that I didn't mean to dredge up old memories but rather get a handle on the background of her story. She took a deep breath and graciously responded. *"I remember the day being cold,"* she went on to explain that it was more of an emotional taciturnity rather than the weather. Knowing that she needed to take care of a 4-month-old and 3-and-a-half-year-old, the biggest issue that concerned her was finances. This concern was for her children as well as herself. She paused for a moment reflecting on the time that we were discussing and elaborated on how much she needed to do and adjust to her life as a single mother.

"What kind of other challenges did you encounter as a single parent?" I continued, furiously scribbling down notes on my notepad. The topics seem to come to her in stages as one led to another. Couple's conversation became irritating and Valentine's Day was the worst. Not having someone to share those (couple's) days with wasn't easy.

Dual parenting was another thing that came to mind, having to be both Mother and Father was also a challenge that all single moms have to face. Another issue, that was very apparent and we both agreed, was that children tend to grow up quickly in these situations. My heart broke a little realizing that, I'm not going to lie. Becoming the bread winner and making sure that her children had everything they needed was at the forefront of her every decision - every day.

Baking cakes became more than 'just' something she did or could do and became Nadia's original entrepreneurial venture ending up being her side hustle when she needed to make a little extra cash. Increasing her network was increasing her *net worth* (Entrepreneur 101), she become known for baking delicious cakes that people could afford as well as create a profit. Thinking back on it, she realized that she could have charged more than she did at the time. She made it clear that knowing her **worth** (we'll get more into this later) and the quality that she delivered, she looked to charge a little bit more and will be doing so in the future, now that she is established. Looking back at it however, she believed that the way things worked out at the time was for a reason and did so because it was meant to be that way.

"What kind of coping mechanisms did you use to get through?" I acknowledged her previous comments and wanted to know more.

"The Church," she answered instantly and continued to elaborate on how the amazing Pastor gave her guidance and words of encouragement that hit her hard and rang true. *She was not alone.* The Church community became more than a way of life or her religion but also became part of the factors that helped her through the days that were hard to face. We all experience them and many people don't have anywhere to turn to. In her case, Nadia had Pastor Lazarus Chetty who did more than preach at a pulpit and go about his life. He actually cared about his congregation.

Food of course became another outlet, as I'm sure many people do. Finding herself in a bubble bath and a glass of wine (not necessarily in that order or together), every second weekend her children would spend time with their father.

It was this time that Nadia used to catch up (or binge) Grey's Anatomy and other series with a decent helping of snacks.

Humour was another coping tactic as Nadia would turn the unfortunate or the uncomfortable into a joke and make light of the situation which though many would see as a band aid, became a method of seeing the funny side of things instead. Taking herself out, reassurance and savouring her time to herself, all contributed to making life just a little bit easier.

"What was one of the lowest moments you felt in the days after becoming a single mother?" I asked. Nadia then told me about the Fiat Uno that she came to possess and the hilarious reaction that her children had upon looking at it. I had to agree with the kids on this one. And though we all know that a beat-up Uno is not ideal, it was four wheels and an engine. She turned to her children and said, *"To you, this is a Ferrari."* I chuckled as she went on to tell me the story of how she was pulled over in that same Uno and the seatbelt was somewhat, dysfunctional. By that I mean the **seat** had broken in half and the situation was quite a dilemma.

The traffic official was more shocked by the state of the seat than the original reason they'd pulled her over in the first place. Looking at the state of things from the outside, the official said, *"But (insert awkward pause) it's in half."*

Besides stating the obvious, the whole situation was quite hilarious to which she can now look back on and laugh about it. We both certainly did.

"What was the highest moment you had in the days after becoming a single mother?" the café was busier now and we continued despite the increased hustle and bustle. A smile crept across her face as a memory arose and she began to regale me in the tale of how by some miracle, she purchased her first car.

A friend of hers worked in the automotive industry and was able to help her with all the paperwork. And after going back and forth, the day had finally come. After picking up the green Chevy Spark, she went to pick up her children from school. The reaction was priceless, *"It's my mommy's new car! It's my mommy's new car!"* I couldn't help but chuckle as she imitated her kid's reaction. After settling from our little giggle, she paused and mentioned that they joined in prayer to give thanks for the blessing they'd received.

I nodded as she went on and told me about how she got creative in entertaining her children over the years and put on shows etc. It was heartwarming.

"What are your hopes and dreams?"

This seemed to catch her attention as she straightened her back to respond. Nadia aspires to reach lofty heights and become more than successful. Her entrepreneurial spirit engaged her enthusiasm as she spoke of becoming wealthy and she expressed the importance of educating her children to be independent.

A glint in her eye arose as she mentioned that her drive and motivation to find a way to make something happen rather than sit around and hope for the best, brought out the same in her children who actually said, *"Mommy, I want to be like you."* Helping others realize how valuable they are and making the world a better place.

"What is the impact you'd like to have on the world? What legacy would you like to leave behind?" my question was the last for the interview and was aimed at not only ascertaining a response but also, it's a question that I believe we should all ponder from time to time to remind ourselves that we are not only meant to pay bills and pass on. After taking a moment to think about it, Nadia looked me in the eye and replied, *"Believe in yourself because, **you are enough**."* She also mentioned how things came together like pieces of a puzzle.

I continued to listen and came to understand the nature of how she'd followed her path which led her to the eventual founding of this organization.

"My life started changing when I realized that I am enough," her words hit a nerve as I paused to let it sink in. I'd encountered many people with the same outlook regardless of their situation, those who felt that who they were and what they were doing, despite how much they did, **was not enough**. Even though it was and they are. Understanding all of that in a single moment is a powerful shift and I realized that people need to hear that more often.

This was Nadia's message to the world.

After many years of struggle, hardship and trying to balance a work-life equilibrium, Nadia was fortunate enough to find love again.

She found someone to walk this path with her coming from the same arena with three children of his own. They met online at the start of Lockdown and got married a year later to the day. One of the main points that she pointed out which grabbed her was the decent conversation as well as the many similarities that they had. At the time that this book is being written, they are purchasing a new home to house their blended family and begin a new adventure.

We concluded our meeting and her message stuck with me, *"You are enough."*

Somehow, I felt that it was something that was necessary for all single mothers to be aware of however, so many others need to hear the same thing and know in their hearts – that they are indeed, **enough**.

<u>Nadia</u>

Michelle

What surprised me most about this venture was the diverse group of women that I'd meet along the way. Even though there were similarities, which we'll get into at some stage, their stories could not be more different, as is their individuality. It was a warm afternoon as I made my way to Michelle's home. I was reminded of spending a lot of time in her area in my late teens and early twenties and pleased to see how the area had developed. Pulling up I saw Nadia's car and Michelle came out to open her gate to welcome me in. She offered a welcoming smile and invited me in, offering a comfortable seat on the couch beside Nadia. I noticed that she took a place on a plastic chair opposite us and Nadia made me aware that she was a bit apprehensive about the interview to start with. I realized that where I was seated wasn't helping matters and asked if we could please swap so that she could be on the couch alongside Nadia and I'd take the chair opposite to be in the "interviewer's" position, so to speak. She accepted and it was Nadia who smoothed things over by giving me a warm introduction and I offered her a brief rundown of who I am and why I was the one in her home conducting the interview.

I felt it would be better to dive right in and allow her to shift her focus which seemed to be the right move because, once she began, I was blown away by what followed.

When most people think of the term "single mom", they immediately think of failed relationships, or divorce. If you use another word that doesn't immediately come to mind because by nature most people don't assume such things, it hits differently. The term is – *widow*.

When I ask my first question of, *"Talk about the day that you realized 'Now I'm a Single mom.'"*, there was a pause in her response since for Michelle, it came in stages and dragged out in a way that would test anyone. She started with the day that she received a call from the traffic department about her car. They asked her if the car belonged to her and responded, *"Yes."* What followed was them informing her that the car had been involved in an accident and that her husband was seriously injured.

My heart sank imagining what that must feel like. Going about your day as if everything is okay then having your world be turned upside down with a single phone call. Her two children were six and ten at the time and became her general main focus.

She continued to explain that she had to *"hit the ground running"* as her new life was seeing to the recovery of her husband who was her best friend and dealing with all that came with being a parent.

I was shocked to find out that his recovery was almost 6 months before he returned home where his care continued.

She was unemployed, tired, frustrated and *"running on fumes"*. After another six months of care, her husband succumbed and passed away.

 I paused for a moment to let that sink in, then asked how all of that felt at the time. She used a word that seemed to be quite fitting, *"Numb"*. She felt numb to the circumstances and the gravity of the situation hadn't exactly hit home just yet. She turned her focus to her children and at the time, she felt as if she didn't have time to grieve.

We went over how tough that must have been and I asked her about how she got on from there. Michelle thought over her responses before she aired them, seemingly reliving the moments and the time of her life. She described it as confusing at first as she went over something many didn't know and I'm sure some who read this would also find educational. When they moved their bond payment of their home over to another, Bond and Home Owners Insurance was *not* part of the deal.

I had to raise my eyebrows to that as Nadia chimed in. In the event of her husband's passing, there was *no* life insurance to provide her with the cushioning needed to get through the trying time.

Her daily life became a struggle for her and her children to keep a roof over their heads.

She continued to elaborate about how the financial aspect was her biggest concern however, when he was around, her husband took care of everything.

And not having him around meant that she needed to carry the load for her family.

At the time of our interview, eleven years had passed since his passing. In those eleven years, Michelle had been working for five.

In the years that followed she dealt with a lot of rejection and distance from those whom she could before rely on. And what she mentioned next became another thing I'd pick up in my later interviews, that she was invited to fewer gatherings or events where couples were present. She mentioned how she felt as if "someone is watching" everything she said or did. The notion sounded a bit ridiculous to me but this was also an educational path for me.

Because she was single (regardless of how), she was placed into the same societal stereotype of a single mother stigmata. The husbands of the women she knew whom she could before depend on to fix something in the house if her late husband would ask were no longer allowed to do so. All because she was – "*single*".

She began to feel guarded and it eventually began to affect her children in the sense that they were also now excluded from these events and gatherings because to invite them would mean their mom would come along.

That struck me deeply as I leaned in to continue the interview. I must admit, my mind was racing at that point as I looked to my notes for guidance.

"How do you cope with the added pressure? What do you do to relax?"

I tried to steer away from the harsh reality of what she had gone through. She perked up and looked around the room which I understood why after her answer. Staying active and staying home, she enjoyed doing things around the house. What I loved also was that she sought to be present in the moment which I knew that many people in this day and age do not even attempt because of the pace of the modern world.

I too am to blame, having a library in my house with a collection of works that would make most Authors envious, I still, at times, found myself scrolling on my phone through YouTube videos and TikTok.

Nature was another aspect that grabbed me which I too like to do on occasion but in Michelle's case, it was her outlet with her children as they found outdoor activities to do together which not only was a great stress reliever but also, it grounded them in the here and now. Since they were no longer invited to social activities, they made their own, getting out and living life in a way that is rare these days. The wind, the ocean, and the greenery of nature did not cost a price of admission and yet, it brought more joy than what most pay a fortune for. Michelle has reminded me that we are surrounded by beauty and yet, we rarely appreciate it.

Michelle wanted to stress a key point, that her children are her *"pillars of strength, on and through this whole journey as a single parent"*. The fact remains that there is constant laughter in their house because of them, which is *"such a blessing"*.

"Can you describe your lowest moment you've felt since the day you became a single mom?"

I had prepared her for the question before I asked it. I had designed them in such a way to access thought patterns that we wouldn't readily use every day and jog the memory somewhat. Her response was not as straight forward as one would think. She went on to speak of the time that she continued to care for her husband when he came home from the hospital and that it certainly wasn't easy. It was hard not only because he needed care, but because it was someone she loved.

The low point came after his passing when the realization sank in that "he's never coming back", "he won't return". This was another jolt for me because we often understand that eventually we all die and we lose people close to us, however, rarely do we understand or fathom the *finality* of death. That person will never be in your presence again.

You'll never hear their voice, or give them a hug. And if that wasn't enough, the alienation she suffered along with her children thereafter contributed to the low point in her life.

For Michelle she could not pinpoint a low point as it seemed to be a low moment in time strung out by a few occasions of feeling at her lowest that would ebb and flow. Understanding that we are not always going to be here.

"Can you describe your highest moment you've felt since the day you became a single Mom?"

I'd hoped to turn the tables and remind her of the moments that kept her going since she had obviously made it through the trenches.

Michelle smiled and went on to let me know that this too was not a single point but a collection of moments spread across her time as a single Mom which I was eager to hear.

She had never shown others what was truly happening, not even those closest to her. She remained strong and never showed others what was really happening within. This is a trait that I must insert here in my studies of humanity which is along the lines of regal behaviour. In other words, this is an act of Royalty.

When she was told by someone close to her that she's **strong** and that *"her children are grounded"* was when she had received the outer validation that she was on the right track. She had *not* been looking for it and she had only been trying to do her best.

And it was a comment that alerted her out of her forward motion to stop and smell the roses of the seeds she had sown to do well. She had done such a great job and it showed in her children which means that it was true. This was something that she had to take a step back for the briefest of moments – and exhale.

"What are your personal hopes and dreams?"

This seemed to stump her for a long moment and she stated that her goal is more about finding herself.

Her main focus was that of her children and providing the structure that they need. She spoke of having to think and be both parents in the raising of her children and *that* I know in itself is daunting. She found herself having more grown-up conversation with them as I came to see that another trait for the children in single parent households tend to grow up faster than their dual parent colleagues. I witnessed it myself as some of my class mates were working long before I thought it legally possible because they needed to.

I grew up on the side of privilege and never knew such hardships until life came in like a sledge hammer to the kneecap.

After pausing and glancing over to myself and Nadia, Michelle said, *"to Live Life"*, which made me smile outwardly and internally.

As I know that I have had moments where I've appreciated life and what it brings, Michelle's goal was to LIVE life. There is something raw in its simplicity. And I'm sure many people go years, without *living* a single day.

"What would be the impact you'd like to have on the world? What kind of legacy would you like to leave behind?"

The question gave us another pause as I'd hoped it would do for all of my interviews since I wanted the ladies to genuinely feel what it was that they wanted to say and Michelle didn't disappoint.

She wanted to be remembered that she did all she could to help others. This resonated with me on a personal level. She was a giving soul and wanted to do the best she could for those around her starting with her children.

"Helping women to find their voice", to know their *worth* and above all, retain and maintain their *dignity*. After that statement, Nadia and I exchanged glances as

we both made the connection from her interview. It was her next statement that hit home as she said the words, "know that *you are enough*".

I got goosebumps and showed the ladies my arms as I tried to contain the chill down my spine. The two had not met in person before that day and the exact same words came out when asked the same question.

You Are Enough.

She went on to mention that even though she would obviously prefer that her husband was still around, she was glad her marriage ended with his death and not in divorce. I nodded as I took in the real essence of the comment.

A final statement she left me with as we ended off the interview was a message that she'd like others in her position to know and that was, *"it's okay not to be okay."*

That message can be used for almost anyone going through trying times however, it seemed to have a special home for this occasion, as it fit in with Michelle's goal to help others, not only single mothers.

I left the property with those words as we waved our goodbyes and it stuck with me ever since.

"It's okay not to be okay".

Michelle

Ladele

I had returned to a familiar area for the next meeting where I had spent many of my younger years and I couldn't help but feel nostalgic as I drove around searching for the next interviewee. I met up with Nadia as we were greeted by a lovely lady who greeted us with a smile and warmly invited us in. We took a seat in her kitchen and Nadia once again gave me an amazing introduction which I tried to follow up with the breakdown of how we'd conduct the interview. Ladele was so pleasant and pumped for the interview that she couldn't wait to get started. I chuckled as I settled in and produced the questions and my notepad to kick things off. I must mention that we did not exactly stick to the script as I allowed her to go off on whatever it was that she wanted to say and tried to throw in the questions that seemed relevant. I did this to maintain the authenticity of her recollection and for her to fully express what happened as she remembered it. And although we at times seemed to jump from timeline to timeline and moved forward and backwards in events, the events were real and hard hitting to the point that I was awestruck that the pleasant and charming lady sitting at the head of the table had gone through everything she was about to lay out.

She had moved back to her mother's house as her marriage came to an end. Her then husband didn't pay for anything and she had to find her way on her own and she eventually lost her job.

Although it fell under what I'd later touch on, she told us about the day she was at her mother's place and was trying to set up the bunk beds for her children when it suddenly collapsed with her underneath. This was her breaking point, her lowest moment at the time.

She had given into social convention that the man would work and provide and that the woman would be the wife and mother and care for the household. The man would take care of things that a man would do around the house and other responsibilities befitting a man, providing and protecting.

One morning while taking her children to school, Ladele was forced to walk the extra distance because she couldn't afford the fare. She walked from Town Center to Westridge as her youngest *moaned* and *"hated every bit of that walk"*, but she forced herself to feel numb so that she wouldn't need to *face the guilt* of letting them walk all the way.

Her marriage was the dream, the goal in life and now it was gone. She remembered thinking to herself one day, *"I need to feel empowered."*

This led her down the road to write poetry and eventually she became a speaker, providing hope for others coming from similar circumstances or simply those who needed it.

She began to take herself out for coffee and began interacting with people. She befriended the staff at the café she frequented and got to know them. Once she could feel what others felt, she *"came alive."*

She had returned from a point of darkness and somehow found a ray of light. The numbness she felt was a daily occurrence and she couldn't identify a point of origin for the pain. She turned to her writing and would like to eventually publish her work. And focusing on herself and what she wanted to accomplish, she began attracting things and people into her life.

Her plan of action was set:

- Find a job
- Move out of her mom's house
- Get her children back.

I could only imagine the heartache she must have endured during that time and as a mother I'm sure Nadia was feeling her pain on another level.

With a small smile she mentioned that, *"at least they were safe."* She noted that when she had to make decisions, every bad circumstance reminded her of the day it all started.

Finding herself in a new area, she found a job and moved in with a man whom eventually, she realized, could not be relied on. The silver lining to that was that she managed to save some money as she worked.

What she said next and what hit me with this interview was that she said that she craved for her children the way others crave *"chocolate"*. What also hit me was that she would pray for something like being able to wash her children's clothes. The reason why this was such a big thing for me was because I'd travelled for many years and took care of myself including my laundry for all that time. And when I returned home for a few weeks at a time, my mom would want to do my laundry and the independent fool in me waited to do my own once everyone else's was done. It hurt.

She went on to talk about how she had trouble being alone and eventually attracted men who she ended up *mothering* and they were all abusive in some way.

It was then that she planned to get out once again and keep moving. Eventually she'd hit a wall and asked herself, *"What the hell is wrong with you?"* which led to feelings of suicide.

Since I was sitting and listening to her, she'd obviously failed in her attempt and let us know what made the change and quite honestly, in some way, falls in line with the teachings of Napoleon Hill and Earl Nightingale.

Setting her alarm for four in the morning, every morning, Ladele would get up to pray. *"I want my family under one roof"*

And using this method of focusing her attention and desire she incorporated the ancient teachings of *"what ye sow, so shall ye reap"*. Her moves became tactical as she then got what she needed to get her life on track.

Ladele sought out and acquired a lawyer, got insurance and then a storage unit in which she'd store second hand furniture. Her job at the time was very accommodating and allowed her some flexi-time to accomplish this feat.

And on a fateful Woman's Day, she moved out. To her surprise she had amassed more furniture than her little storage unit could handle but made it work. Ladele had done so well that she had to give stuff away as she worked to improve and gain a good credit rating. She became strategically deceptive and kept telling herself, *"I can, I can."*

Instead of letting things get to her she became like rubber and let things or issues bounce off of her as she kept moving forward.

She remembered the words of her mother, *"Be patient my child."* And her patience certainly paid off.

To get her child into college, Ladele called them up, got the paperwork and walked to the institution and handed it in herself. She was always so giving and had begun to take care of herself.

Her time was now. She had gained the momentum she'd needed to build the life she'd wanted. It was her time.

She had felt like she was losing herself. She went on about how she'd gotten through those times and shared a piece of advice that Nadia and I took on board. *"Tell yourself you are so sorry."* She told herself that she is so sorry and had to forgive herself. She realized that if she doesn't take care of herself, she wouldn't be true to herself. *Self-care is not Selfish.*

"How do you cope with the added pressure? What do you do to relax?

Ladele is quite artistic. Besides writing, she enjoyed her woodwork and crafts. We were eventually treated to the fruits of her labour looking at the interesting picture frames and other artistic products around the room.

"You need a skill," she added as she continued to speak about how she grew from strength to strength in her independence.

"Can you describe the lowest moment you've felt since the day you became a single Mom?"

She elaborated about the fact that her oldest daughter was her biggest concern being a victim of circumstance and surrounded by people who *"indulged in substance abuse"* as well as forgetting all the help she as a mother gave her in times of need. When things were at their worst, it was her mother, Ladele, who was at her side. I noted how it was a common trait with human beings as we treat those closest to us the worst and we treat strangers with respect.

"The spiritual stand point is real," she added. We nodded in agreement as she spoke of her belief and how it got her through.

Again, I was reminded of how prayer had directed her thoughts and emotions in the direction of what it was that she wanted to achieve and happen in her life.

"Can you describe the highest moment you've felt since the day you became a single Mom?"

Moving into her current location (which was quite nice actually) after bringing her things out of storage. That was a day that would live with her forever and be a source of joy and freedom. She had finally gotten to a point of freedom. She had choices and this gave her confidence.

The jobs that she had, had also contributed to her skill set and allowed her to grow as an individual and as a woman.

"What are your personal hopes and dreams?"

Ladele thought about this for a brief moment and answered that her dream would be for her children to *"see her and drink from the fountain of experience and knowledge."* I scribbled furiously to keep up with her and nodded in agreement. She wanted to prevent her children from experiencing the same that she went through.

I thought that this is what a parent would want for their children and although that would be obvious to most, many parents don't entirely live up to that. This mother was driven by the need to see her children thrive. I admired that and believe that, *that* ideal should be respected.

"What would be the impact you'd like to have on the world? What kind of legacy would you like to leave behind?"

She responded to this faster than I expected and had to jot down what I heard as fast as I could. She wants to touch as many people as possible and help them understand what they are going through. She was brimming with ideas and wanted to see them realized and receive the justified recognition for them.

I soon understood that her journey had come full circle and gaining her freedom and confidence had opened up a whole new world of possibilities in which she was able to spread her wings. Digitally this was in the literal sense as she connected with a young man on LinkedIn and arranged for him to teach her how to create and start a website.

After some time had passed, Ladele now has regular virtual meetings with the Director and CEO of a Software Company to do their marketing. This was a part that I found most impressive given the story I was being told.

She had literally wondered from place to place and at times did not know where she would sleep or find a meal. Ladele was the embodiment of a self-made woman.

She wanted to show others where she came from and to know that no matter what happened in life, "it's going to be okay."

"When the enemy is around you, lie still. It's okay. It's going to be okay."

The following is the poem written by Ladele as a coping mechanism to deal with the trauma of her past. I hope you read into the truth hidden in plain sight – as well as the hidden truth that floats barely beneath the surface.

It's Mine…

Gracefully, I carry myself…

Pretending all is fine –

Joking and laughing, pain hidden away.

Don't want to share it, it carries my name

I own it, Its mine

Don't like it, but it's fine.

I understand now…

It molds me to life's finest design…

Beats me like a punching bag, throws me against the wall

Picks me up and throws me down,

Ruthless and unkind!

It speaks no word to my defense

Its only aim is to offend…and leave me lying on the ground – Just to return again

With yet another blow it comes to tear my heart apart,

My blue and purple skin reflects his aim to bring me down,

And yet my soul he tries to take with influence of words…

My spirit is what angers him…with that… He's not content.

<u>*Ladele*</u>

The Group Discussion

The group of ladies I was to meet and conduct a group interview with was comprised of a group of ladies from Undercover Heroes. Each unique in their own way and I was concerned that I was lost as I searched for the location. I had arrived somewhat early and it turned out to be good because my navigation had placed me on the other side of the tracks and thus, in a different area completely.

After solving my directional woes, I communicated with Nadia and I was assured that I had in fact arrived at the right location. The plot was large and exceptionally clean as we made our way to the living room where we were to conduct the group interview. The ladies settled in and chatted as I once again positioned myself on a stool to face them. They smiled broadly and laughed as Nadia made her introductions as did I. Feeling very welcomed and at ease, I felt that we were about to have a great discussion as I took the situation as a great learning opportunity.

When I was younger, I sat in the company of girls who had forgotten my presence and I learned more about women in twenty minutes than I had in twenty years. I'm not exaggerating.

One of the girls was laughing at the discussion and flicked her hair only to discover that I was next to her remarking, *"Oh Duane, I forgot you were here."*

They all laughed realizing what I'd just heard and I quietly sipped my beer and processed what I'd just learned. This was different of course. I was now a man and still, I had a lot to learn as I believe that every day is a learning opportunity. We settled in and I decided not to follow conventional line of questioning since my other list was intended for directly personal stories and I was in the company of six women in the same proverbial boat. So, I devised a set of questions that would address the issue in such a way that the ladies would have their say in a general sense.

As an *outsider*, so to speak, I tried to come up with a list of questions that someone in my unique position would ask given that the ladies I was interviewing actually wanted to have their story told but also wanted to clear some things up and have certain misconceptions addressed. Some things stood out as a trend as I discovered with other ladies I'd interviewed and some things were news to me. All of course was completely relevant and I was honoured to be a part of it.

Let's begin…

I purposefully asked this question because I wanted to see if I was right about the pattern and indeed, I was. Almost immediately one of the younger Moms piped up and mentioned that old chestnut, the Stigma. The branding we as a society place on the Single Mothers that they are only out to find a father for their children and this is their sole aim in dating or goal in life. Now let's not forget that there are women who do date men with the intention of finding a man to fulfill the role of husband and father and some have even shamed a man for not wanting to do so and said that he's not *Man Enough* to pick up the mantle. That doesn't mean of course that *every single mother* is only looking for a man to be *that* man. The group I was in the presence of all nodded as she spoke of occasions that the wives of her friends and colleagues would give their husbands and boyfriends a hard time for knowing or even talking to them out of the *irrational fear* that as a single mother, she's out to *steal* her man.

"Labels," another lady mentioned and she went on to explain that they are no longer daughters, sisters, or women. The Label they are stamped with is that of Single Mother and nothing more.

I thought back to a single mother I worked with and over a few drinks she had told me about the realization she'd had that although she was a mother, she had to remember that she is also, a woman. I stewed over that as I listened intently. The others chimed in stating that they receive friend requests from men and get told that because they are the single moms that it must have been them to initiate the interaction. But of course. Because men in relationships don't initiate connections with other women, do they? (Insert sarcastic tone here) "How naïve," I thought out loud which got a chuckle out of the group.

Then when they see these people or go to events or any other place where they'd have to interact with these men then they'd have their guard up.

The other issue is the way their relationships fell apart if at all. As I stated with Michelle before, not all single mothers are single because their relationship fell apart.

"Who cheated?" was what they blurted out and the rest chimed in as they carried on about how that's how some people reacted when their relationships ended. *"No. Everyone breaks up because someone cheated,"* another lady added, her statement dripping in sarcasm and they all agreed. I had to agree as well of course having gone through something similar in my previous relationships.

I can't guarantee that my exes never cheated on me because I know that some did however, that was not always the reason some of my relationships ended. Sometimes, people just don't fit. They discover more about each other that doesn't make them happy and many, don't want to put in the effort to make it work.

"What kind of changes would you like to see in society with regard to the treatment of single mothers?"

There was a short moment before a woman who had not been as vocal as the others decided to speak up and tackle that one. I turned to face her as she spoke of the fact that single women take care of themselves and that comes across as them being perceived as they are on the *hunt* so to speak. The others nodded as I asked the rest of the group if this was the case. "No one will ever really know," she continued when she spoke of the inner struggle that they go through on a daily basis and then put on a brave face for the world to see as they handle their own business. They value themselves in the way they carry themselves. It was a common thought that women in relationships and marriages tend to let themselves go and not take care of themselves and use the fact that they are taking care of their families and men that they are allowed to do so.

Some women felt that because they were in a relationship or marriage that they no longer needed to maintain their appearance or beauty since the game is now won. They have the man and the child or children and this was a license to pay less attention to their own upkeep because they are too busy taking care of their family.

Bear in mind that not all women are this way. I personally know women who are in the gym more than I am and they are wives, mothers and professionals in fantastic shape.

I speak of the misconception of the women who are not maintaining their own appearance and accuse the single mothers of maintaining themselves to be *on the prowl* searching for other women's men (heaven forbid, any man).

Another lady interjected and also clarified that looking good and getting *dolled up* was also a coping mechanism to feel better about themselves regardless of whether she received the attention of others or not.

To round up that question, they wanted to be clear, that the last thing they wanted from the general public or society was pity.

I nodded and appreciated the candor as they clarified that people think that because they are single moms that they are now helpless and need to be pitied. Everyone in this world needs help now and again. Simply because they are single mothers doesn't mean they should now suddenly be pitied for their apparent affliction. One of the ladies fixed her hair said, *"I'm fine just as I am."*

"If any, what are the benefits of being a single mother?"

Some smiled and chuckled as I'm sure if they hadn't heard the question before they probably already knew the answers.

"A man already knows that you can be a wife," one of the ladies answered. It was a passing point but good to know for any men searching for that kind of thing. If she had the house and her own income then it was an obvious bonus but the other main point was that sometimes people in general want their own time to themselves and besides their children, they have their own time, to themselves. The collective agreement was that single mothers had less stress and could form their own life and steer their own lives.

"How hard is it for single mothers to date? What are the differences from dating when you're single?"

"We have a buffet of men," one of the ladies pointed out and though this was met with a chuckle it was a good point.

Besides the men who already had wives or girlfriends, there are still single men out there, millions of them. Being a single mother, she will select her man while considering that this decision will affect her children.

The subject was brought up of how things changed with the fathers of the children as well. After they separated or got divorced, the fathers were still quite active in their children's lives. However, one participant commented, that once he got re-married, things changed.

I could tell that her mind was remembering scenarios and situations that came to mind to spark the statement and she elaborated. Things that he normally would have done including coming around to see his children, he was no longer *allowed* to do. She continued to explain that when she would reach out to him about things that involved the children or the house that needed his attention, his new wife would say that his ex-wife is making things up, manufacturing things out of the ether to get him to come around.

I shook my head at the absurdity of the notion but then again, a part of me knew that there were women who did do that deliberately to sow discontent in the home life of the men who'd wronged them and moved on. I get that it happened but to judge all ex-wives by the same measuring stick was wrong. I've been placed in the same bucket of cheaters and players simply because I'm male. I understood what it was like to be accused of things you haven't done or to be judged based on the actions of others.

In another case, the men cut themselves off and only spoke directly to their children which created the atmosphere of the mothers feeling like *they* were the *intruders*. What also created even more conflict was that in some occasions, the new wife would be antagonistic towards them however, the former in-laws still treat them as family and in some cases, *better* than the father's new wife. I started feeling for these guys who had to go home after a session like that.

The picture was painted that they would arrive at the venue, looking presentable and well kept, then be treated like a long-lost relative who's come home and the family would fawn over the now single mother and ex-wife as the new wife would pout in a corner over the family's treatment of her. It was an issue.

"How does being a single parent affect the children?"

The parents helped a lot in raising the children. I actually came to realize in that moment that I hadn't thought of the parents in the prior interviews. I leaned forward with an adjusted sense of focus. They were thankful for the help their parents provided and they were grateful. I nodded in agreement.

The ladies mentioned in the same breath about how they had to practice tough love with their children and in that respect, the children grew up with strong character and a lot faster than most.

I thought back to prior interviews as that seemed to be another pattern where the children had to adjust to their lives as their parents either split or they had lost one entirely. I could only imagine what that was like and felt a silent moment of gratitude in that moment. The lady closer to me who'd been a bit more silent than the rest mentioned that Grade nine or ten was the time when their children became a bit more rebellious.

The rest of the ladies agreed and nodded and murmured in unison. *"Without guidance, children tend to drift"* another added and we all agreed with that point. Another point was brought up that in some cases, living conditions were poor because they were single. One of the ladies mentioned that she went into a state of depression because of it.

I admired where they all were, given where they'd started. The more vocal of the group voiced her point that she hadn't fully processed the issue at first and some of the ladies seemed to resonate with that as I looked around to gauge their reaction.

We circled back to the point that children grew up so fast and at times, they did so because they *"didn't want to bother Mom."* The older daughters took on the role of Mother to ease the pressure of the single mothers as the big sister's moved on from the situation and took care of their younger siblings.

A sullen vibe descended on the room as one of the ladies said slowly, *"You feel a sense of guilt, when you realize what you've done to your kids."* They threw in comments about how they became even more protective over their children as well as the children themselves looked out for each other.

The issue of the pandemic and COVID – 19 brought up the fact that some of them had to break the national regulations to feed their families. I felt that one and the harsh reality of how the lockdown had affected us all in some way or another but for some it hit harder.

A topic was then brought up that answered a question I'd had on my mind for years. One of the ladies explained that when something went wrong in their lives, it was like a switch that activated the original reason why she was in this mess and she'd relive it all over again. I looked around and it seemed to be a common feeling.

Not all could afford it but some of the children ended up with psychologists which seemed to help a great deal. And one of the main points that they wanted to make was that even though there were clearly issues between them and their exes, they never bad-mouthed each other to the children. That I can respect.

"What makes single parenthood special?"

The immediate response I got was that they were *"better off alone."* One of the ladies said emphatically that she missed nothing about being married. They didn't have married couple arguments, they didn't need to put up with the moods and overall, they had all the freedom they could enjoy. The way they explained it was that, they didn't have to be *that person* for everyone else anymore. They are people too. Recently they'd held an event where one of the single father's made a rather good point and said, *"Let's talk to each other and not about each other."*

Everyone nodded in agreement that they shouldn't assume they knew what others were going through. Not dealing with their partner's insecurities was another point which I jotted down and acknowledged.

"As a group, what kind of shared goals can we all agree on for ourselves and our children?"

The general ethos was that they wanted to teach, train and help others who found themselves in their position and have no idea who to turn to or what to do. Empowering others to do what needs to be done and contributing to growth, mentally speaking.

To be Happy, Single or Married. I nodded to that one and listened to the others mention that you need to *"forgive yourself"* as well as others. A feat far easier said than done as I tried to process that in my mind and soul.

They mentioned that they have trouble growing in their career as they were constantly tired and burnt out. We all know that getting ahead in your career meant putting in more than what was required and as a single mother, it gets hard when you have both roles to fill. They became too busy for life in general which directly affected their children. There was also a guilt that was placed on what they were trying to do in getting ahead.

This was where the forgiving yourself came into play. *"There's no manual for becoming a single parent."*

"How would you like to help others in your position? What can we all do, as people?"

To my surprise, one of the ladies mentioned that she would actually like to get married again. I was happy to hear that even though it wasn't the overall opinion.

"We'll figure this out together," I heard one say as I wrote and chose to keep writing and capture those exact words.

"There's nothing to be embarrassed about," another said and there was an audible agreement from all in attendance.

"Don't be afraid to ask for help," I heard another chime in and we all nodded at each other as they went on about the group that they had formed and how the floor was always open for questions.

"Empower yourself," I wrote it down as it was said without looking up.

"Get some independence," I heard the words and scribbled it down while the group went on about the various skills, they as a group, had acquired to up their game in taking care of business.

And to end off the talk, a message for all in the same position, *"You are not alone."*

The rest of the session was spent chatting about general things and what their plans were for future events. The hostess served refreshments as we laughed and relaxed now that the main interview was done.

I was pleased to have been a part of the meeting and as we said our goodbyes I felt as if I learned a lot and got to know the ladies even though a few hours before, we'd never met.

The drive home was a silent one as I processed the information and I mulled over the reality of the world we lived in. So many things were just that much harder for some and many things some take for granted which others would die for.

Generally, I'm grateful for my life and thankful for the basics. I once wrote a post on social media saying, *"If you have a roof over your head, food in your belly, a warm bed to sleep in and running water, you are blessed."* I am thankful for that every day, and as I stepped on the accelerator, I was thankful for my fortunate upbringing. I quietly thanked my parents and family. My life was a blessed one.

Nicolette

Not all of the interviews could take place in person. My next interview was to take place over the popular video conferencing web application called Zoom. I understood that we all had lives and I actually lived a fair distance from many of the ladies I was meant to interview. The video call proved adequate as long as I was able to continue and not have too many internet drops and other interruptions which came with load shedding and poor network service. Which, even though I had a Fiber internet connection, still seemed to less reliable than good old fashion WIFI.

I waited for the call to start and got my coffee ready (as you do) and placed myself in a rather comfortable seat in my lounge. I didn't know that I was going to be sitting on the edge of it for the next hour as I listened to the young lady telling me her story of how she overcame incredible odds, did what most thought impossible, is still doing what she set out to do and helping others along the way.

Nicolette, or Nicky, had also gone through a similar path as Michelle of losing her husband as he passed away in 2016. She did explain that even though he passed away then, she was on her own – long before that.

Nicky has a daughter and a son and around 2007 – 2008, her son was diagnosed to be on the Autism Spectrum. Now bearing in mind that many parents do take the news harder than others, her ex-husband took it far worse than most.

I felt for her as I adjusted the screen to full view and increased the volume not noticing before that it wasn't even close to maximum. I had been raised to treat all with compassion and respect and I was no stranger to those on the spectrum though I didn't actively know anyone who either was or family of someone who was. I listened intently as she proceeded to describe how it would be the end of their relationship as she knew it and his spiral into the abyss that would eventually lead to his passing.

From the time that they received the diagnoses, Nicky felt like she was on her own. In many ways, she was. From 2008 onwards, she spoke of the trouble she had adjusting to what needed to be done as well as navigating through her new life. She needed to be all that she could be for a child that would need special attention and she was doing it alone. I wrestled with the idea of her coping with her daughter as well as a child who, which she would then go on to explain, was on the low end of the spectrum.

She now found herself in the work space for children with special needs.

It was a long and arduous journey and she managed to find a way. I pondered on how much effort and determination that must have taken to get her to where she was now. Respect was the word that came to mind.

She paused for a moment before continuing about her ex-husband. He was a good man, but the news hit him hard. They were married in the year 2000 and working in the IT industry, he had a good job with a stable income. With respect I asked about how it got to that point or which vice he chose and she answered, *"Alcohol abuse."* She elaborated about how he would drink to deal with their situation. Losing his job was only a side effect and in 2011, the divorce was finalized.

I was pleased to hear that in 2012, he got back on his feet and she had gotten back the man she married. Sadly, he relapsed and eventually entered rehab. I have known and dealt with many people who have either used some form of drug, including alcohol and required the love and support of their family and friends to get them to rise above it. I understand that as a qualified Life Coach that eventually the patient or client, will have to decide to change or stop what they're doing in order to move forward. It's exactly the *leading the horse to water* analogy. People need to have to make that decision on their own no matter how much love support and coaching you provide.

I've lost clients simply because I told them that. I have the game plan set out, but it is *they* who have to take the necessary steps to make it work.

In 2013, Nicky started the Centre for children with A.S.D (autism spectrum disorder). The name of the facility is **Autism Connect Learning Centre** which I discovered all over when I Googled it and though small, is doing some amazing work. I looked at the images online and read up on what she's done after the interview and I was even more impressed. We talked a bit more about how the center was founded and the effort she had to put in to make it happen. I was truly inspired and respected the way she charged forward with a goal in mind. I'm that way as I'm sure many people are, but she did clarify that it was her son who was her true inspiration and drive for doing all that she did.

Nicolette founded **Autism Connect Learning Centre** in 2013. It has since then grown and evolved into a recognized and best practice Centre for learners in the autism spectrum. Currently it has 25 learners with a full staff compliment including support staff. Autism Connect will also be celebrating its 10th year anniversary in 2023, a significant milestone indeed.

"What was your biggest concern in the beginning and what did you do to tackle it?"

Nicky was silent a moment and I'm sure thought back to the days she scrambled to get everything in order with the added responsibility of having to care for a special-needs child.

She told me that juggling work and family was what came to mind initially however, her ex-husband's relapses were also a major concern. She felt emotionally cut off during this time and was also criticized for being civil.

There were times that she had to leave him with the children and even remember him saying something to the tune of, *"What, don't you think I can take care of my own children?"* She returned to find him drunk and her child playing with scissors. I cringed at the thought and was thankful that nothing happened. We continued.

"What kind of various challenges did you have along the way?"

Nicky mentioned something that I noted as part of the trend or coincidences (not really coincidences) that she didn't have friends. Her mother loved her ex-husband and once again she brought up the point that she was criticized by others for being civil with him and the situation. But in explaining the story, she pointed out that it was a matter of, *he had no one else.*

Nicky then brought up one of the main issues that I'm sure most of us think of first in this kind of situation, finances. Her son needed private therapy and it wasn't cheap. It was only a matter of time before she went into debt which also became another source of stress.

I am no stranger to that financial monkey on the back and understand how it can weigh on the mind. For a brief moment I thought about how bad this cycle of financial issues keeps so many people from achieving their goals. I guess I was about to be proved wrong.

"What do you think are the main struggles, that are unique to single parenthood?"

She sighed heavily and responded that being a single parent is hard. Seeing to everything on your own that a parent needs to see to, the primary concerns of being a parent, even basic needs become a struggle.

"It's draining," she said as I thought about how it can be that way for all single parents and then on top of that she was constantly thinking of issues that needed her attention.

Taking care of her children, her ex-husband's vices and working to pay the bills as well as find the treatment needed for her son – she was always, out of time.

"How do you cope with the added pressure? What do you do to relax?"

Nicky had to admit that she didn't have a real social life. Her life revolved around work, her children, spending time with her sister and attending the occasional event.

She smiled and mentioned that she took up invitations when she could, which wasn't much.

They go to the movies, spent time outdoors (I nodded and smiled at that one) especially on weekends. A joyful smile automatically crept up her face as she told me about how she would plan outings and took her children for ice-cream, the St. James Walkway in Muizenberg and enjoyed the air. I may have been taking notes but I was also inwardly envious that I had not planned to do the same things which were in the same city and I hadn't been there in years. I made a mental note to do so. (I still haven't).

She perked up as she thought of another thing that she loved to do with her children and for herself which resonated with me on a personal level.

Nicky frequently visited the famous *Houw Hoek Inn* and explored the Elgin region. I felt a twinge in my gut as I told her that my family is from and some still are in the Elgin area such as Botriver, Grabouw and Caledon. I loved the Houw Hoek Inn and their pies are legendary. We both gushed over the sites and activities that are rare gems which many South Africans enjoy, not only tourists. My parents included who also like to do as Nicky does and stay a weekend or so at the Houw Hoek Inn. Nadia giggled at the two of us digressing over this particular topic and I voiced my regret that it's been a while since I've gone there for personal reasons.

They both nodded and Nicky insisted that I "make a plan" and get up there as soon as I can. She elaborated some more about how beautiful the area was and how rejuvenating the experience is, even if it's a few days. I agreed completely and thought of the spectacular view and memories of my childhood. It really is remarkable.

"Can you describe the lowest moment you've felt since the day you became a single mom?"

I knew that it was a major shift in the mood and I tried to ease into it. Nicky paused and replied that she felt *lost*. The feeling of not knowing what tomorrow would bring was the worst.

Living day to day and taking every day as it comes was her torment. The year 2021 was the worst for navigating life as she had a health scare which put a lot of things into perspective.

The business life in general as she ran the Autism Learning Center became so hard that in 2021, she truly felt like giving up. I exhaled as I could only imagine what she must have been going through. Having all of that to deal with after going through everything she did then, focusing on what needed to be done. They found a growth which needed to be looked at in more detail. It was this scare that made her realize that she had lost herself. Nicky mentioned something afterwards that I had heard before and had to learn the hard way as well. The saying was that, *how can you take care of your family if you don't take care of yourself.*

I whole heartedly agreed. Thankfully, the biopsy proved to be benign but this scare brought her life into perspective as she then drew up her Last Will and Testament. That shook me. I had not even considered it and I still haven't, even though I know that I really should.

That was a true moment where she had to consider life and death – and face it. She wanted to serve her family and her community and she began working with a Life Coach.

I smiled and brought up the fact that I was one too which Nadia reprimanded me for not bringing it up. I had to chuckle at that one.

"Can you describe the highest moment you've felt since the day you became a single mom?"

This was the question I'm sure she was subconsciously excited about as I would have been because of its legendary nature. The ASD space is where she found herself after effort and study and without a tertiary education, she managed to pull it off. Founding the Autism Connect Learning Centre was one thing but it opened her up to the world of the Autism Global Community. What followed was amazing by no small measure as she was able to completely change her world and travel to Houston Texas, USA to attend the World Autism Organization in 2018, an event with workshops and speakers held every four years. She met amazing teachers and educators at this four-day event filled with doctors and professors held at the Marriot hotel.

This event would truly be life changing as she met a woman named Charlotte from Zimbabwe whom she formed a true friendship with and would also invite her to do something she'd never thought she'd do.

Nicky stayed in Cyprus, Texas for a week and made connections with people who are now close to her heart. She was able to present what she'd learned and was suggested to attend and speak at a conference in Kenya in 2019.

I was blown away by the journey that she had experienced and currently still riding the wave as she'd gone from not knowing what the next day would bring to traveling to the United States to attend a function and then be one of the speakers at an event in Kenya. That is truly spectacular.

We all gushed over it for a few moments as Nicky relived the times she'd experienced and went on about the people she'd met. I could picture the place she visited by the way she described it and wanted to be there given the description. One day perhaps.

"What are your personal hopes and dreams?"

Not surprisingly, Nicky would like to travel some more. Not only to visit the people she'd met but also see much more. She'd gone from a suburb in Cape Town, to Texas to Nairobi. I'm not surprised that she wants to do more, it's called the travel bug I believe.

She also would like to remarry. A point that I jotted down immediately since not all of the ladies I'd interviewed felt the same way.

Nicky added that she'd like to finish her degree in Public Management and then go for her Masters in Business.

I had to applaud her tenacity and perseverance. Her drive to ascend to the next level had to be commended as she sought the next ceiling once she'd broken through the former. I have to tip my hat at such resolve in the face of such adversity.

Nadia also commented on how her persistence was not a common trait and this led me to my next question.

"What would be the impact you'd like to have on the world? What kind of legacy would you like to leave behind?"

Nicky was silent for a moment and I eagerly awaited her response. *"Never give up,"* she responded. I nodded and captured that in real time. She advised that being consistent in your efforts means that things have to eventually change for the better. She wants to know that she's made a difference in this world but especially, for her children.

We each have an amazing story and hers was that she wouldn't know what to do if she didn't have Autism Connect. To have made such a difference even in a single lifetime.

She'd like to think that she's done what she's meant to or purposed to do. And her last messages she wanted to leave with us was, ***"Do what you need to do, don't give up."*** The Book of Esther is what she goes by and to remember that timing is key. I took that the moral of the Story of Ester was to always do the right thing by using all of your resources and position to help others. A fine lesson I'd say.

Nicolette

Rosebud

My second interview over Zoom was to be with another extraordinary woman who would teach me a lesson in humility and strength before the end of the evening.

Rosebud is an example of self-made in every sense of the word since the true test of someone's mettle is to strip them of everything and see if they can once again rise to the top. It's like the rich mentality as they say that some people can be completely wiped out and build themselves up once again while others remain defeated. Rosebud is the former.

I was greeted by a welcoming smile and charming chuckle as Nadia sang her praises in her introduction. I was eager to begin and find out the next exciting tale which would contribute to the collection we were putting together.

Strong women they all were but that wasn't the point. It went far deeper than that. It was about finding the strength when that was your only option and persevering when the odds were stacked against you. Rosebud was ready for my questions and so we began.

"Tell me about the first day that you realized, 'Now I'm a single Mom.'"

Rosebud tilted her head and explained that hers was a rather unique situation since the answer would be two-fold. She had become a single Mom – twice. I was shocked to put it mildly as I scribbled down *'2x single mom'* on my note pad and waited for her to elaborate. Rosebud had been married with 2 boys and after eleven years of marriage, they got divorced. She recalled the day as she loaded up all of their clothes into the car and the bed on top. Fortunately, there was a house where a resident was moving out for her to move into. She looked up and said that she thought to herself, *"It's now up to me."*

Six years went by and she eventually met someone else and they got married. The product of their marriage was a baby girl, that was ten years ago. I waited for more as I clicked my gel ink pen which was clearly flowing a lot faster on my note pad and made me take my time in listening and taking notes. The second marriage unfortunately ended with his death by car accident. I could feel my heart sink at that moment and respected that she was reliving this pain all over again.

She made a point which I don't think about since I'm single, but when she needed to fill out some forms at work, she now had to tick off the box that said – *widow*.

"What was your biggest concern in the beginning and what did you do to tackle it?"

According to Rosebud, the first time was the worst because she was literally starting with nothing. She thought mainly of the protection and nurturing of her children and she made it very clear that she didn't want to become a statistic. I keep mentioning that these women are strong and brave however, I got the sense that Rosebud was one that was that way before she needed to go out and find it. I didn't know if I was right, it's just the vibe that I got. You pick things up along the way and this is something I sensed in her.

She went on to state that she didn't want to stand in the way of her children and their father. Even though there was always some conflict because, he didn't support them or help in any way. Even though this was the case, she didn't stop them from seeing him or being a part of his life. I respected that since I know it's not always the case and many women literally use their children as bargaining chips. The women I've interviewed are not so. The direct opposite in fact. I thought back to the discussion where the ladies mentioned that they wouldn't even bad-mouth the father to the children regardless of his involvement. I nodded and listened as she explained the complexities of their situation.

The second time she was made a single mother, she had to tell herself that she's survived this before and she'll survive it again. This time she was stronger. She sang that part actually and we all had a chuckle.

She smiled as she said that it was a strength that her late husband had taught her and that made me smile. She actually thought that if this event would help others, then *so be it*.

I saw how she had made peace with his passing as she went on that his presence was a *gift from God.* And what struck me even more was that in the days leading up to his passing, she could tell a difference in his behaviour or demeanour. She honestly believed that he knew that his time was coming soon.

That blew me away in a manner that I have trouble describing. And I'm supposed to be a writer.

"What kind of various challenges did you have along the way?"

Financial troubles came to mind off the top of her head. I nodded knowing that it's a major issue regardless of your circumstances and even worse if you have less coming in and more mouths to feed.

She had trouble with this aspect because she wanted to do more for her family but was limited. I got that and felt a familiar twinge in my chest.

She explained that as a single parent, you have to figure these things out on your own. I remember what the group mentioned about how there's no guideline or manual to being a single parent and people have to learn on the fly.

Another point she brought up was that society tries to get into your business and that's where the judgement comes in. I inwardly cursed the status quo of shaming people regardless of their circumstances. We shouldn't have any right to pass judgement on any one and yet, we do so on a daily basis.

We've made it a societal norm to judge others based on their circumstances, appearance, status and of course, colour.

Rosebud went on to clarify that she didn't feel the need to explain herself to anyone. Nadia and I shook our heads approvingly in agreement.

She told us a story that I could relate to, of how people receive messages through songs, conversations and in this case, announcements where she heard a preacher say, *"I will fight your battles for you."*

Sometimes you receive guidance or reassurance from these moments that seem coincidental and yet, are too close to be a coincidence. I believe that the universe is too mathematical to make mistakes.

"How do you cope with the added pressure?"

There was a brief humming to which Rosebud told us that Saturday was her *rest day*. She would watch TV to gain inspiration and made it clear that self-care was in the interest of self-preservation.

I always like to think that Self-care is not selfish and people looking out for themselves isn't necessarily a bad thing. Like the other ladies mentioned a few times, if you don't take care of yourself, who will take care of your family?

She enjoys going out with her children and spending time with them in general. She had to make the time to do so as her children hated her being busy.

"Can you describe the lowest moment since the day you became a single Mom?"

The time that she had to grieve for her late husband was definitely the lowest she explained.

I sat back in my chair and absorbed the moment listening to how she talked about the time after he passed away. *"He's gone,"* were the words of realization that he would never return. She said it was more grief than despair. I listened intently as she told us about how it took a while for them to get back to normal life. Her sons truly stepped up and took care of their sister.

It was as if they'd matured overnight and became the pillars of support that she needed in her time of need. I loved that and Nadia nodded as well, we both thought about how this was yet another trait in the story of the children of single parents. They grow up quickly.

I've been told that sometimes we find the strength to do what needs to be done because we don't have a choice. I guess that's the norm for the children of single parents. It's reality and her sons were up to the challenge.

Can you describe your highest moment since the day you became a single Mom?"

Rosebud was and still is a woman of faith who prayed and in prayer, she asked to be rewarded for her faithfulness and effort. She could not have written the script any better than the way things played out thereafter. She received a job offer which increased her salary dramatically and it was not long after that, she was headhunted for a management position.

We all gushed over the strength-to-strength situation we were hearing about and I love a story of triumph.

She mentioned that the way things turned out, she could only attribute it to God as she said, the way it happened was clearly a way that higher forces were at work.

She was intentional with a childlike belief.

When something happens that she's prayed for, then she chooses to believe that it's the hand of God at work.

"What are your personal hopes and dreams?"

Rosebud wants to be a speaker as well as eventually write a book. I smiled at that one and threw in my offer of assistance in the production and advice to get it done.

She is currently satisfied with her job but there are other things that she'd like to do such as:

- Have monthly meetings with women
- Have them talk freely
- Share their stories and learn from each other
- If need be, take it to Zoom and do so virtually

I loved the ideas and Rosebud and Nadia went off on getting this set up and pursue her wishes. I agree that it was a necessary action given what I'd learned.

I believe there were ladies who needed the guidance of others in their position as well as, there were some who simply needed to be heard.

"What would be the impact you'd like to have on the world? What kind of legacy would you like to leave behind?"

She was silent for a long moment before methodically answering, *"irrespective of what happens, it does not change who God is."* I agreed and captured the statement in real time as she dropped another classic.

"Tough times don't last, tough people do."

She wanted to be used by God and be an instrument of purpose. She did not want *to be defined by the things that have happened* in her life. Her message to others is that one should not define your life by the moments of pain and suffering. Too many people become stuck in their own *pain*.

I sat in awe as I felt like I was witnessing the end of a Ted Talk as she continued.

Those moments are meant to make us stronger by going through the pain.

"Let the fire refine and not scorch."

<u>Rosebud</u>

Joan

I was greeted quite pleasantly and it was a warm day. Nadia was already there and I was more than impressed by the décor as the councilor spoke of how she'd modified and decorated her home over the years. The living room where we'd be seated for our interview was spacious and beautiful. Her dog was too adorable as he took his place under the table and I unsuccessfully tried to pet him.

It was my first time meeting a Ward Councilor and I had an idea that this would be yet another interesting and epic tale. I guess the old adage of *be careful what you wish for* played some kind of role here.

We would jump around a bit with her story and when the questions feature, I'll be leading with them.

I could not have predicted the tale that I was privileged to hear. The greatest story that was never told, until now.

"Tell me about the first day that you realized, 'Now I'm a single mother.'"

Joan started off with letting us know how it all began long before she would get to the stage of actually being a single mother. It wasn't like most cases and warranted a bit of a back story.

She was forty-two at the time his infidelity occurred. She took a pregnancy test in the year 2000. Just to be sure, she took the test 3 times. The father was not exactly happy as she would soon discover why. Her oldest was a daughter and had run away. She didn't get along with her father was an understatement of note. He began to distance himself and eventually they were separated.

His girlfriend was a married woman as well which made the entire situation quite complex and I struggled to keep up with it all.

In October of 2001, her water broke and she had to drive herself to the hospital where she gave birth in the hospital corridor. I couldn't believe what I was hearing and my overactive imagination painted an intense picture like an episode out of a medical drama series.

She was pleased to find flowers to welcome her home as well as the plans to build a holiday home and renew their vows.

Things would change though a few years later as one day she drove by and saw his car parked at the house of the other woman.

In 2003, the Sherriff handed her the divorce papers. He was estranged and in 2004, the court date arrived.

Being a police officer, he carried a gun. She had come home to find that he had shot through her dresses where her heart would be. She *felt nothing.* I struggled to process that bit of information and really couldn't believe what I was hearing. She clarified that once he left, he left for good.

Joan began to describe how her daughter got involved in the criminal underworld of Cape Town and began to associate with the top of echelons of the Capetonian Gangs. She got involved in the drug scene and the trouble went from bad to worse. The relationship with her policeman father, they believed, was linked to her lashing out and rebelling against authority along with all that the lifestyle promised. Unfortunately, that has an extreme downside.

In February of 2006, her daughter was shot. I almost dropped my pen even though it was established that her daughter was still around, she must have survived.

Her ex-husband's reaction was what hit the hardest as his words rang true. She looked us both in the eye and said, *"If you live by the bullet, you'll die by the bullet."*

We paused over that for a short moment before proceeding. I had a sudden urge to stroke the dog at my feet, he was still guarding his mom and wouldn't budge. Rejected again.

During the years this was happening, her daughter had given birth to a baby girl and left her child with her grandmother. At times they didn't have food for everyone but somehow, she made it work, as I've come to believe, the name of Nadia's organization was aptly named, Undercover Heroes.

Joan mentioned that she was actually abandoned at the age of five and the woman that raised her was the neighbour. She remembered back in those days; the aunties of the neighbourhood were the unofficial babysitters as the community looked after their own. In this case however, the mother never returned and the Auntie took the child in to raise as her own. The home she grew up in was crowded, but she had a roof over her head. After creating a life of her own and looking back at all that's happened, she slowly looked up and with the softest gaze she said she wouldn't change a thing.

Religion and faith therein seemed to be at the core of many of the successes and achievements of the women I'd interviewed and the councilwoman was no different. At her first prayer meeting, her daughter ended up forgetting most of her past and asked for the forgiveness of her father.

I was aware of the concept that people in groups focused on a single goal would alter the collective consciousness and every individual had their own experience. This was the case for this situation.

In 2014 she became a commissioner of oaths to my surprise as she brought to our attention that it turned out to be a major benefit because in 2015, Joan was heard as a speaker in her community and was asked to be the Ward Councilor. Of course, one thing led to another and she was successful. We shared a gleeful chuckle in quiet celebration.

We blended the other questions together as she described that her biggest concerns were for that of her children. She had no other concern beyond that and honestly, that tied into everything that goes into it. Finances and other similar issues that come with the struggles of being a single mother were what bothered her in the beginning. Now however, that was all behind her.

"How do you cope with the added pressure? What do you do to relax?"

Her face lit up as she went into the detail of preparation and hosting of Sunday lunches with her family. The food and cakes (her cake is amazing but we'll get to that) and having all of her family over. I thought back to the days when my family did the same and how much I enjoyed it.

Her pictures were her hobby or source of happiness and I was honoured to see them all. The memories she held on her walls would last forever and I could feel the welcoming vibe as I looked around the room. She had truly made it a home and I could sense it.

"Can you describe the lowest moment you've felt since the day you became a single mom?"

She looked down and was silent for a moment. Joan then went into detail that her daughter had survived after multiple suicide attempts, being shot by the police and having been sent to prison several times. She received a phone call in March 2013 that she had to come through to Rondebosch, which changed their lives forever, unaware of the condition she'd find her daughter in. She had received several calls that her daughter was no more, the verse in Isaiah 30 V 15 stood out, **"...in quietness and trust shall be your strength."**

She had prayed over her daughter's body until she gasped for air. It's moments like that, that my belief in miracles is renewed.

The story was one of wonder and would restore faith in the most cynical of people. I sat in awe.

"Can you describe the highest moment you've felt since the day you became a single mom?"

Her beaming smile had returned as Joan told us the day that she was announced to be the Ward Councilor. She called her daughter and even received word from her ex-husband. I imagined how proud she must have felt on that day. Given the twists and turns her life has taken and the ups and downs her family had gone through. She had been abandoned as a child, had a tumultuous relationship with her ex-husband and family to become a ward councilor of her community. I was proud for her.

"What are your personal hopes and dreams?"

Joan expressed her interest in writing a book. I was thrilled of course and we spoke briefly about how we'd get it done and if she ever needed guidance. I had a book that we discussed which she would be able to go through and get it done.

I found it wonderful that the ladies wanted to write their stories in their owns words. And with that. I looked forward to the final question.

"What would be the impact you'd like to have on the world? What kind of legacy would you like to leave behind?"

Like some of the others I'd interviewed, I felt that this was a question she had been waiting for. She straightened her posture and her look become firm. Making eye contact with both of us, she began to speak, *"Never allow your past to determine your future."*

"I've never allowed the dust to settle on me. I've always risen before the dust could settle."

Those words stuck with me for the rest of the day and once we'd concluded the interview, we spoke heartily about life and other things. Joan then whipped out the cake I spoke of before. A cold drink followed and the deliciousness of the cake made me forget that I'm watching what I eat. It was worth it.

I learned more about her family as she elaborated that even though she'd been abandoned by her parents, in 1990, she took her father in to live with her.

Fearing the turn of the Millennium, her father had a heart attack and passed away on December 31st 1999 while they were attending the midnight service. While living with her sister, her mother came to visit her for a few days in January 2011, she called Joan to pray for her. She called the ambulance, and on her way to the hospital her mother was *"called home to be with the Lord"* on January 8th 2011. The verse which spoke volumes for this moment in her life was Exodus 20v12, *"Honour thy mother and father and your days will be long."*

We spoke more about her son who had traveled and his marriages both in South Africa and abroad. She was always present through those events and her experiences being there was quite exceptional. Her family was tight and they were together (minus her ex of course).

She had extended family as well including those in need and those who simply needed an ear. A mother to all is the term I would use. A kind soul who would do what she could for those in need. Truly – an Undercover Hero.

Joan

Duane

I've always prided myself on being a lifelong learner. Being open to new information and new experiences has landed me in some sticky situations at times however, I've also managed to grow. Taking that approach has allowed me to grow far more than if I was the kind of guy who only went to work, paid bills and watched Netflix on weekends. I read a lot, I study new subjects and have more certificates and qualifications than I can use however I don't regret any of it. Learning something new is a path to brain longevity I've been told.

Walking into that room and answering that *call* (literally and figuratively, pardon the pun) eventually lead to the culmination of this book. I have written nonfiction books before and interviewed hundreds of people and in my years of being an Author I'd never gone through the rollercoaster of emotions that I'd gone through during the interviews which I conducted in preparation for this book. A rollercoaster may be cliché however, there's no other way for me to really describe it.

I met wonderful women who welcomed me into their homes, whether physically or virtually and I was not prepared for how it would affect me.

I designed the questions to take the ladies back to the moments which these events took place and to have them tell me their story. Being an empath turned out to be a double-edged sword as I felt what they felt however, I was then able to convey that in my writing since I felt it as if I was there, in the moment, watching the scenes unfold. It was intense.

I am truly grateful for the opportunity to participate in this venture and after the journey I believe that I'm a better man for it.

A large part of the lessons I've learned was that there was a trend with how single mothers are treated and perceived.

- Single mothers are seen as *"out to get a man"* whenever they come out and women want to keep their husbands away. It's preposterous.
- Single Mothers take care of themselves and are happy with themselves which translates into them glowing and being radiant at times and that, to others, translates into *"they doll themselves up to steal men"*. Ridiculous but it's a reality that others feel this way.
- Once people hear that a woman is a single mother they immediately assume, *"Who cheated?"* I'm not even going to give that any energy.

- People come up with stories and theories about single mothers because they are single and there's a societal stigma attached to them for being single. They are then watched and their every move is questioned and scrutinized because people (especially other women) assume that they are up to no good and can't be trusted.

I wanted to address this issue for a moment and give my short point of view. There is a psychological opinion that people who accuse and point fingers are actually the guilty parties and trying to label others to defer the attention from themselves because it's easier to judge others than look inwardly and honestly evaluate ourselves. I am trying really hard to live a life without judgement which makes me a lot happier and less burdened by the issues and opinions of others since what other people think of you is none of your business.

I have to thank all of the women whom I've interviewed and of course, the founder of Undercover Heroes, Nadia. This has been an extraordinary experience and I look forward to future endeavours as I can only learn more than I already have which I can list as follows:

From **Nadia** I've learned that no matter what you go through, *"you are enough."*

In the face of the worst tragedy imaginable, **Michelle** taught me that *"it's okay not to be okay,"* when things get hard. We break down, get back up and keep moving forward.

From **Ladele**, I learned that you need to be patient and remain focused on the end goal. *"When the enemy is around you, lie still. It's okay. It's going to be okay."*

From the group discussion, I learned many lessons however, the main take away that I was taught was a message they wanted to convey to the women in their position but didn't have their support structure, *"you are not alone."*

In my first virtual interview, Nicolette taught me that in the face of adversity and when the circumstances seem to be against you, *"Do what you need to do, don't give up."*

In my next virtual interview, I met Rosebud whose story also blew me away given all that she went through and being made a single mother not once, but twice, I was taught that, *"tough times don't last, tough people do."*

After been taken through the motions and riding the wave of circumstances that Joan had gone through to rise to the position of Ward Councilor, I learned a valuable lesson, ***"Never allow your past to determine your future."***

I spoke about how single parents pull off amazing feats to accomplish what couples do on a daily basis and many of them still complain about getting it done even though *they* have their partner next to them. We have to admit that getting the job done with one arm tied behind your back is hard. I'm not saying that being a parent is an easy task at all, don't get me wrong however, couples have each other to lean on and single parents have themselves. Finding the strength to keep going for the sake of your children, I can respect that. I always have. Though now, I respect it from a whole other standpoint and I am grateful.

Thank you.

Duane Carter